The She Approach To Starting A Money-Making Blog

ANA SAVUICA

DISCLOSURE

The information in this book is heavily based on personal experience and anecdotal evidence.

Although the author has made every reasonable attempt to achieve complete accuracy of the content in this book, they assume no responsibility for errors, omissions or for how the reader chooses to use this information.

The author cannot guarantee results or any specific out-comes gleaned from using the methods outlined in the following pages.

***

Affiliate disclosure: This book contains affiliate links. Any purchase made through such links will result in a small commission (or referral fee) for the author, at absolutely no extra cost for readers.

The author only recommends products that she personally uses and/or genuinely loves that are essential to start and grow a profitable blog.

CONTENTS

INTRODUCTION

So you want to make money blogging…

Well, you've picked the right book! Because not only will I show you how to start a profitable blog, but I'm going to share with you what it takes to make money online without selling your soul, and how to get paid for your hard work, creativity, and unique skills instead.

Sound good? Brilliant! But before that, allow me to introduce myself.

My name is Ana and I am a blogging growth strategist over at The She Approach (www.thesheapproach.com) where I help bloggers get started, increase their traffic and their income, so they can turn their passion into profit.

Starting my own blog back in 2016 was one of the best decisions I've ever made and monetizing it has allowed me to craft a life I love, work on something that I'm truly passionate about, have flexibility and control over my own schedule, travel and visit my family more often (without worrying about money).

And it also allowed me to get and raise a puppy by myself (because I was able to work from home a lot more than before) – which is by far the best thing about my lifestyle.

The success of my blog was not immediate or easy, but it was a thrilling journey that I got so much out of (and I'm not only talking about money, but personal and professional growth as well). And my biggest realization? I've discovered that even if you don't earn a full-time income blogging, the added money can still change your life.

It was during a spontaneous trip back home to see my family in October of 2017 when I earned my first $1,000 in a week which I earned 98% passively (everything was either scheduled or systemized beforehand), leaving me to enjoy my time home without any disruptions.

I was blown away that something like that can even happen, especially since I was only blogging for a year (along with having a full-time job and being a full-time student at the time).

Later on, in the summer that followed, I was able to pay for a 10 days' blogging trip to Portugal, using money that I earned while blogging part-time. (And here's the mind-boggling thing about that – I made the money to pay for everything, except the flights, in one single affiliate campaign that lasted no more than 8 days.)

Achieving that level of success with a relatively new and small blog has given me a taste of what's possible. And ever since, I've dedicated myself to finding effective strategies to grow my income and help others do the same.

I truly believe that there is enough success to go around in the blogosphere and I want to help you get a piece of this pie as well! If you want to know how my blog has been doing since I started my journey you can check out my income reports by going over to www.thesheapproach.com/category/income-reports/.

So while I had to take the long road when it comes to learning how to monetize my blog (you know... the road full of dead ends, frustrations, failed attempts and wasted time), you don't have to! This book will provide you with a roadmap that will:

- Help you set up a professional website from the get-go.

- Help you make your first few dollars as soon as possible.

- Show you what your next steps should be in creating a profitable blog.

If you want to get started right away, check out my tutorial on How To Start A Blog In 3 Easy Steps over on www.thesheapproach.com, under the "Start a blog" tag. It includes a few screenshots and technical walkthroughs, along with some strategy that will be helpful, but everything else is also covered in the following chapters.

One of the main reasons why I'm writing this book is because there is a huge misconception flying around the Internet that you need a huge following and a super-popular blog to monetize it, and that couldn't be further from the truth.

If I had waited for that to happen, I would still be waiting right now and I would've missed out on a lot of money and on a lot of opportunities to help other people as well.

Because here's the truth: my blog is still not a very big deal in comparison to other popular bloggers out there. But I probably earn more money than some of them by simply having a better monetization strategy and a growth plan.

That's what I'm good at, and that's where my book is going to be different from a lot of other similar blogging resources out there.

But please, keep in mind that this book is not a get-rich-quick scheme, and what I teach in it will take time and effort. You will not become a full-time blogger overnight and there are no shortcuts to this (besides having a great strategy that will save you a lot of wasted time!).

I can only teach you what I know (and what I've learned the hard way) – and that is how to start a PROFITABLE blog that will excite you, open up new opportunities and help you out financially.

But if you want your blog to bring a profit, you have to be willing to commit to these three things:

- Commit to finishing this entire book (without skimming over the "boring" bits).

- Commit to investing a little bit of money to get you started the right way (after all, profit equals earning more than you spend, not earning without spending a dime but – I promise – there's no other business model out there that has the potential to make you so much money for so little investment).

- Commit to spending a few hours each day (or at least each week) working on your blog and bringing your idea to life.

Can you do that? Can you commit to make your blog a success? Because once you finish this book, it will all be in your hands!

If so, I am so honored to be a part of your journey! I've included everything you need to know in this book (brace yourself – it's a lot), but if you want to ask me something specific or you need more support, I'd love to hear from you any day over at www.thesheapproach.com.

CHAPTER 1: SETTING UP YOUR FOUNDATION

INTRODUCTION

My guess is that if you're reading this right now, one of the following scenarios applies to you:

- You have this brilliant idea for a blog already burning in the back of your mind, and you've decided what you want to write about and what you have to offer to the world, but you're not sure it's going to earn you money or HOW it's going to earn you money.

or

- You're still uncertain about what you want to write about or what your blog's focus should be, but you know that if you're going to put your time and effort into it, you want it to be profitable.

So, if you fit into any of the two categories above, this chapter is going to help you either refine your idea (and validate that it can be profitable) or help you come up with an idea from scratch for your first money-making blog.

By the end of this chapter, you should be crystal clear on why you're starting your blog and what your blog will do, not only for you but for your readers.

Because here's a hint: if you want your blog to be profitable, it should do way more for your readers than it does for you!

But more on this later. Right now, let's focus on finding and refining that idea!

KNOWING YOUR WHY

Why do you want to start a blog? It's such a simple question, yet so many of us don't stop to question it when we get struck by the inspiration to start one.

What is your "why"? The driving force behind this new project? What's your true motivation? What will keep you going when things get hard or when you feel like your blog is failing?

Because that's going to inevitably happen and what differentiates bloggers who make it from bloggers who don't is grit - who is passionate enough about what they do (and especially why they do it) to show perseverance and keep going?

And if you don't have a strong motivation behind it, a conviction that, no matter what, you need to make this work, then I'm afraid that this blog will only be an occasional hobby.

So I want to challenge you to make a list of 3-5 reasons why you want to start this blog and to write them down. As long as they motivate and excite you, there are no bad reasons!

For example, you can start a blog as a creative outlet that will allow you to share your ideas with the world. Or perhaps you have a unique insight into a topic that other people are struggling with, and you really want to share what you know, help and educate others (or even inspire them!) and make a difference.

Or perhaps it all boils down to the fact that you want to make money online, become location independent, be able to work from home, contribute financially to support your family, quit your day job, spend more time with loved ones, be able to travel more, and so on.

Make sure to jot down your responses, make them as specific as you can, and pay attention to see if a little fire gets ignited in you when you're thinking about your goals. (If not, you need to think bigger!)

Note: Starting a blog to make money is an amazing motivator, but I found that adding at least one "why" that's targeting a bigger, deeper purpose (such as helping others or making a difference - however small - in someone's life) will make you more likely to follow through with things, believe in the work you do, be determined, consistent and create an awesome blog!

FINDING YOUR BLOGGING NICHE

Now that you know your "why", and you know what you want your blog to do for you, it's time to spend some time thinking what your blog will do for others - starting with your blogging niche.

A blogging niche is simply a way to describe the topics that you blog about, and a way to categorize your blog according to the relevant industry, to make things easier for both your readers and your potential collaborators to identify what you can do for them.

Here are some popular blog niches and ideas for you to consider: fashion, beauty, lifestyle, travel, fitness, weight loss, health, mental health, investing, budgeting, personal finance, interior design, homemaking, parenting, kids, birth, DIY, crafts, blogging, business, social media, relationships, hiking, self-improvement, food & recipes, technology, and so on.

The ideas are endless but it all comes down to what you have to offer and what you're passionate about.

There's been a lot of debate online about whether you need a specific blogging niche to have a profitable blog, or if you can just write about everything and anything under the sun. And I want to approach this subject because I feel like that's where a lot of bloggers (myself included) start off on the wrong foot.

I personally believe that if you want your blog to have the potential to make a full-time income, then **you need to have a well-defined blogging niche**, even if you narrow it down to 2 or 3 main topics (such as a budget travel +

personal finance blog, or a blogging, business + technology blog).

The idea here is that you don't want to spread yourself too thin, and blog about 10 different topics because you're going to have a harder time building a loyal audience (especially if they are only interested in only 1 of those 10 topics) and establishing any sort of expert status.

Think about all the big bloggers and personalities out there! Most of them are known for their expertise in 1 or 2 topics/industries - unless their personal brand is what they are known for (think celebrities!) and then they get away with more because their fans are interested in all facets of their life.

Narrowing it down to 2-3 topics that you're most passionate about can be the difference between your blog making it, and your blog just confusing people.

If you want to help people lose weight, then blogging about fitness and beauty and travel and finance and your dog and your favorite nail polish is just going to be confusing. But if you start a fitness blog, where you talk about your journey and include workout tips, recipes for healthy meals and even some activewear fashion posts, then they all tie together nicely and they are all relevant to your readers and your blog's mission.

So while your blog topic should be easy to describe to people when they ask you what you blog about, it doesn't have to be on just 1 super-specific topic (unless you want it to), as long as it addresses the needs of a well-defined audience (more about this in the next chapter).

For example, when I started in the blogging world I had a lifestyle blog and I covered everything from recipes to fashion, student life and dog training tips. Honestly, I was all over the place and I was getting nowhere fast with my blog.

It was just a jumbled mess of everything that was going on in my life, and I didn't really stop to think if any of it was useful or of interest to my audience.

When I rebranded, switched my focus and narrowed down the topics that I wanted to blog about, the growth of my blog started accelerating.

All of a sudden I was able to clearly communicate not only what I was blogging about, but what I can offer to my readers and who I'm speaking to. And you wouldn't believe what a difference that made!

Just keep in mind that when you're trying to speak to everyone, you will appeal to no one.

So don't be afraid to pick a focus, because with clarity comes progress.

***

There's also a misconception going around online that only certain niches and blog topics can make money.

And while there's some truth to that just based on the opportunities that exist out there in terms of monetizing, I also know bloggers who blog about crocheting and flooring that make way more money than traditional "money-making" niches.

And that's because it all boils down to your strategy and the way you choose to monetize your blog.

That being said, if the blog topic you choose solves a problem for someone (even if it's something like helping people save time, organize their house, lose weight, be more productive, learn a new skill, figure out what to wear or where to travel), then it can make you money.

Ideally, this would be a problem that people would be willing to pay to solve or an area in their lives that they normally spend money on.

For example, you wouldn't think that make-up necessarily solves a problem, but people still spend good money on it if it's something they are passionate about. (Fun fact: the global cosmetic products market was valued at $532 billion in 2017.)

So if people resort to looking online for solutions to that problem, or there's a passionate group of people surrounding the topic you want to blog about (think about fishing and other hobbies that people want to learn more about), then you're halfway there.

Note: There are still some niches that are very hard to monetize because of the nature of the topic they cover or the few opportunities out there to work with brands or promote products. (Think about grief, divorce, certain medical conditions, and so on.)

If you want to approach a more unusual niche, and you're not sure if it's going to make you money, do some research on similar blogs out there and try to figure out (or reach out and ask the blogger who runs it) if they are making money.

Even if they aren't, read the last chapter of this eBook to find out which ways you can monetize such a blog.

For example, I know a mom blogger who created and sold courses, and even started a membership site aimed at parents of kids with autism, taking a hard-to-monetize niche and transforming it into an online business that brings together a community and actually makes a difference.

So don't dismiss any ideas until you've thoroughly thought it through.

**

So, if you haven't already decided, here are a few more things you need to consider when choosing your blog niche.

First and foremost you must love the topic you choose. If you are an accountant (so you have the expertise) but hate your job, then don't start an accounting blog! You're going to have to write about the subject you choose for years and you will have to write tens if not hundreds of blog posts on the topic.

So whatever you pick must set your soul on fire, get you excited, make you curious and you must not dread writing and thinking about it.

 What could you talk about for hours without getting bored? What's one topic that lights you up when it's brought up into a conversation? What makes you curious and what do you love pondering? Write down a few ideas!

**

Second of all, you must think (objectively if possible, but without being too hard on yourself) about what topics you have some real insight into and expertize on. If you love fashion, but don't really know anything about it (or if you aren't curious to learn more), then that's probably not a good topic for you.

Could you give a 1-hour presentation on any of the topics you've just written down without any preparation? Then that's your sweet spot.

A few other questions that can help you determine if you could contribute helpful and insightful content on those topics would be:

- What's the one thing you always get asked about?
- What do people in your life come to you for advice for?
- What are the areas that you want to learn more about and that you're endlessly curious to dissect?

Because here's the thing: you don't have to be a certified expert on a topic to write about it and you definitely don't need a degree to really make a difference in other people's lives. If you are even a few steps ahead of others, you can help them get to where you are!

And if you've been through something and managed to conquer it, or you know more than the average person about a certain topic, you need to use that!

Write down a few topics that you know a lot about and that popped into your head as you were reading this.

And now, to find the sweet spot and decide on a blogging niche, you need to look at both of the lists above and see if there's any overlap.

The sweet spot for the perfect niche is a topic that you love, that you have some expertize in and that there's a need for (a problem that your knowledge can solve and that people are willing to pay to make it go away).

All in all, don't put too much pressure on your niche early on (you can always change it down the line, like I did, because sometimes you simply can't know until you get started) but try to have an idea of where you want things to go and who you want to serve.

If you've found that your blogging niche sweet spot contains 2 different subjects, and you can't pick between them, combine them but don't over-complicate things.

For example, you could have a crafts and cooking blog. But don't overdo it by adding a third unrelated topic.

IDENTIFYING YOUR TARGET AUDIENCE

We have already established that if you want to start a money-making blog, then you have to solve some sort of problem for a specific group of people.

It doesn't have to be anything life-changing but, ideally, it needs to be something that people are willing to pay money to make it go away or make it better.

If it saves people money, time, frustration or it helps them achieve a goal (it helps them make money, learn a new skill, clean their house, get their kids to stop throwing tantrums in the cereal aisle, train their dog to behave or help them make shopping decisions online), then you're on the right path.

If your blog only acts as a diary and it's all about YOU, you're probably never going to make any real money from it. (Unless you are already famous, in which case, people might actually be interested in what you have to say.)

Over the last few decades, the landscape of blogging (and that of successful blogs especially) has changed from online diaries with personal anecdotes to content creation that brings value and solves problems (which goes hand in hand with the information age we live in.)

Your blog's content needs to be focused on helping others solve their problems, or it needs to speak to their interests. And to do that, you actually need to know who you're targeting (who you're trying to help), so you can anticipate and identify those problems and help them solve them.

This is why it's crucial to know who you're writing for - who your target audience or dream reader is, as we're going to refer to them in this eBook. Because they are going to set the tone for everything you do on your blog, including your blog monetization strategy.

So, who are you writing for? Is it busy moms? Homeowners? Pet owners? College students? Women who've been through a break-up? Etsy shop owners? Fitness junkies? Single dads? Fiction authors?

Who are they? What are their problems? What do they value? What do they struggle with? What makes them happy? What are their interests and hobbies? How do they spend their money?

Look at your chosen blog niche and think about what kind of people will go online searching for solutions or help in the area that you're an expert in (and on the topics you're planning to write about). Be as specific as you can, and try to construct a profile for your target readers.

If you're a beauty blogger, your audience could be women between 18-28 who have acne and need skincare tips. If you're a finance blogger, you could target self-employed adults who need help budgeting so they can save for a house. And the list goes on and on and on.

But before you move on, it's crucial that you take a moment to reflect on who your target audience is. The more specific you can be, the better clarity you will have when it comes to growing your blog and making money from it.

This will also set the tone for what type of posts you're going to write, what you want to be known for online and how (and where) you're going to reach these people.

Above I included just a few of the things that you need to know about the future readers of your blog.

In time, you might develop a better understanding of who is attracted to your blog and you might even learn to recognize their struggles and problems better.

(Pay close attention to the comments and questions you get, because that's your audience speaking to you!)

But until then, try to gauge who they are and speak to people in your life who fit those criteria to understand them better.

For example, if you've decided you want to start a blog aimed at single, working moms, speak to 1-3 single moms that you actually know and compile a list of 5-10 questions to ask them that will allow you to find out more about the struggles, dreams, and habits of your target audience.

This is basically blogging market research 101, and it's the foundation of every successful monetization strategy. So don't skip it!

NAMING YOUR BLOG

Having an idea of what type of blog you want to create and who you're targeting is especially important now because it will determine the first step you're going to take into taking this idea and transforming it into something tangible: your blog name.

Once you've decided on a niche, topic or multiple sub-niches, your next challenge is to come up with a blog name, one that is obviously not already taken (or doesn't infringe on existing trademarks that big brands own, so make sure to double check).

Ideally, you want the name to reflect your blog's purpose, speak to your target audience and allow you to cover all the topics you're planning to write about in the future.

(You don't want to choose a name that's going to narrow your creativity or discourage you from exploring your industry further.)

For example, my blog name allowed me to move on from a lifestyle blog to a blogging strategy blog (without having to change my name as part of the rebrand) because it represents my approach, and even if that moved from general lifestyle to blogging, it still applies.

It's almost like my blog name has taken life as a brand of its own, and this allowed me to explore and make changes to my vision, instead of having to start from scratch.

I want to challenge you to have a brainstorming session once you've set your mind on a blog topic and write down 5-10 different blog name ideas.

Once you do that, you can easily narrow it down by checking to see which names have already been taken, and asking friends and family to vote for their favorites or simply go with your personal favorite.

If you're still struggling to come up with ideas or narrow it down to one name, I invite you to read my blog post on How To Choose The Perfect Name For Your Blog over at www.thesheapproach.com/how-to-come-up-with-a-blog-name/ where I talk about a few strategies that I and other fellow bloggers have used to find that winning blog name.

COMING UP WITH A TAGLINE

So far you should already know the following things about your blog:

- Why you want to start it
- Who you want to help
- What type of content you want to publish
- What you're going to call it

To help tie everything together, and to give you a sense of direction (and a sense of belonging for your readers as well), you need to come up with a short mission statement (or tagline) that you can use to explain what your blog is all about and to help your target audience connect with you straight away.

For example, my tagline is "*Empowering women to build digital empires*" and I've recently made it even clearer, so when I describe what I do online I say "*Helping bloggers increase their traffic and income*".

Although taglines are not mandatory, when your blog name is a little more creative or it requires some explaining, having a sentence there that will inform people who have just discovered your website is essential.

When somebody lands on your blog, or hears your mission statement, you want them to feel like "Yes, this blog was created for me! This is just what I need".

Because that's how you get them to stay on your blog longer, join your email list and become raving fans!

***

So have a brainstorming session and think about one sentence that would best describe your blog's mission.

Here are a few examples of some taglines that work really well:

- *Making a hectic life healthy* (fitness blog aimed at busy millennials)
- *Learn to travel. Travel to learn* (travel blog)
- *Smart ways to live a passive income lifestyle* (money-making blog)
- *Helping you lose weight, get stronger, live better* (fitness blog)
- *Create your best life and mommy like you mean it* (mommy blog)

And the list doesn't stop here. Your tagline could be informational (telling readers what your blog is all about) or it could reflect your personality and humor, attaching a unique feel to your brand and making you more memorable online.

If you're struggling to come up with ideas, look at some brands out there that you love and see what marketing slogans they are using.

What do you love about their mission statements? What stands out to you?

Use them as inspiration and try to come up with a unique sentence that you think would appeal to your blog readers and would encompass the work you're planning to do online.

CHAPTER 2: SETTING UP YOUR WEBSITE

INTRODUCTION

Starting a blog today, technically speaking, is easier than it's ever been. While a few years ago you had to know how to code to be able to build a website or hire really expensive designers to have a professional-looking blog, now there are systems, platforms, and templates that you can use to start blogging without having any coding experience or web design skills.

That being said, there is still a learning curve to getting used to certain blogging platforms and the entire concept can be a bit scary if you've never dabbled in anything similar before. But trust me when I say that you can start blogging without ever having to become a tech expert.

I have built not only a blog but an online shop for bloggers – www.bloggingmode.com all on my own and that's because I found the easiest (and cheapest) way to create a professional website. And this chapter will teach you exactly how you can do it as well, so you can have your blog live by the end of the week (even if you have never owned a blog before).

***

Before we begin, I want to point out that technically, the cheapest way to start a blog is to use a free blogging platform such as WordPress.com or Blogger, but if you want to start a money-making blog, I advise against it.

This is the part where you have to invest a little bit of money, but trust me when I say that I only recommend things that are absolutely essential to buy if you want to profit from your blog. And I know this because these resources helped me make money blogging.

Investing in my blog early on has motivated me to see things through and take my blog seriously.

From personal experience and, from what I see from other bloggers all the time, if you start a free blog you're going to give up on it sooner rather than later. Take it from somebody who had 3 free blogs that never led anywhere.

Cold hard truth alert: with thousands of bloggers out there, if you really want to stand out, you need a professional self-hosted website (which I'm going to show you how to create in this chapter).

Free blogs never get as far, and they don't even come close to the same earning potential. And that's not going to change anytime soon.

BUY BLOG HOSTING

If you're serious about starting a profitable blog, you need to acquire blog hosting and become a self-hosted blogger.

Unlike free blogs, that are stored on the platforms you create them on (and over which you don't have much control), hosting allows you to safely start and store a website on specialized servers and build a professional-looking website with your own domain address.

So instead of having a WordPress blog with their name and branding, you are renting a virtual home for your blog where you get to control everything!

If you are unfamiliar with the terms of "web hosting" and "self-hosted blogs" and you want to understand them better before you start your blog, here are a few posts that explain this concept in more detail:

- What Is Hosting And Why Do Bloggers Need It over at www.thesheapproach.com/what-is-hosting-and-why-do-you-need-it/
- 7 Reasons To Go Self-Hosted With Your Blog over at www.thesheapproach.com/7-reasons-go-self-hosted-blog/

But basically, you can't start a professional blog online until you pay for hosting. Luckily for bloggers, there are plenty of companies out there that offer really affordable rates for the price of a Starbucks coffee a month.

My favorite hosting company and the one that I've been using (and loving) for the past 2 years is Bluehost. You can start your own blog with them for under $3 a month, using my unique discount link:
www.thesheapproach.com/bluehost.

Here are just a few reasons why you should pick Bluehost to start your blog with as well:

- They are the number 1 hosting company recommended by WordPress.

- Despite the really affordable prices, Bluehost offers a better quality of service than other (cheaper) companies which means that your website is going to move faster, perform better for SEO and more. Even WordPress endorsed them as a trustworthy hosting source.
- They offer a free .com domain name (so a custom URL for your blog such as www.thesheapproach.com).
- They offer a free SSL certificate (Google will mark all websites without an SSL certificate as not secure, so this is essential to have on your blog.).
- They offer free WordPress integration and installation (it only takes one click!)
- Their customer service (in my experience) is great and their team is always ready to help via live chat.

If you're ready to start your blog or go self-hosted with your current free blog, you can read my full tutorial on how to start a blog over at www.thesheapproach.com/how-to-start-blog-2018/ (I update it yearly) or simply go to www.thesheapproach.com/bluehost and follow the instructions there to set up your website.

I wasn't kidding when I was saying that it's never been easier to set up a blog, and this process proves it. (Bluehost makes it really easy as well!).

SETTING UP YOUR WORDPRESS BLOG

One of the other reasons why I love Bluehost is because they allow you to use one of the best blogging platforms out there - WordPress - for free and set it up with a single click.

WordPress acts like a back-end editor for your website, allowing you to customize the appearance and the content of your blog without having to know any complicated code.

If you've owned a free WordPress blog before, it will look pretty similar, but now that you're self-hosted you will be able to:

- **Choose and upload a custom-made theme** instead of having to choose one of their free themes that thousands of other bloggers have.
- **Choose from their database of 40,000+ plugins** (most of which are free) to further customize your website and add additional features.
- **Monetize your website and expand your reach**. While free WordPress websites don't allow you to place ads (but they take advantage of your visitors by showing them ads anyway and

collecting the profits), a self-hosted WordPress site allows you to make money online on your terms.

There are a lot more benefits to running your website through WordPress that I'm sure you'll discover down the line, but let's get back to what matters: setting up your WordPress website.

If you followed the previous steps to buying your hosting from Bluehost, you will be able to automatically install WordPress on your new website and manage it from there.

Once you've done that, you can start building your blog and changing the theme around so it looks just the way you want it to! Pretty much everything is customizable and can be changed with a few clicks.

***

Choosing a premium WordPress Theme

The free WordPress themes that you can choose from their library can be quite tempting, but no one ever said: "*I'm so happy I went with that free theme*". In other words, you want your website to stand out, to be unique, memorable and professional, and a free theme doesn't do that.

Luckily for us, there are hundreds of already designed themes waiting for us out there, ranging from feminine and professional to minimalistic or intricate.

All you have to do is find something you love! WordPress themes tend to cost between $30 and $100 (I found some amazing ones for less than $50) and you only have to pay for them once.

Here are a few places where you can find stunning themes (along with shortcut links towards them):

- **Bluchic** - www.thesheapproach.com/bluchic - An independent WordPress theme shop with stunning designs.
- **Pretty Darn Cute Designs** – www.thesheapproach.com/prettydarncutedesigns - Sleek and girly designs for the ultimate female orientated blog.
- **Restored 316** - www.thesheapproach.com/restored316 - The ultimate vault for beautiful WordPress themes.
- **Angie Makes** - www.thesheapproach.com/angiemakes - More stunning and unique WordPress themes.
- **Creative Market** – www.thesheapproach.com/creative - Another huge marketplace for themes

that cover a variety of styles and needs (such as themes for e-commerce websites, blogs hosted on different platforms than WordPress and more).

Looking for more ideas? Check out my post on 10 WordPress Themes For Female Bloggers & Entrepreneurs (type in www.thesheapproach.com/wordpress-themes-female-bloggers/) to find my absolute favorite themes for bloggers (along with detailed instructions on how to install them on your blog).

And voila! Your website will be modeled after the theme you chose, and you will be able to easily make the changes you want to personalize it.

ADVANCED WORDPRESS HELP

Now that your theme is in place, your WordPress website is ready to be customized and filled with content.

But first, you need to learn your way around it. If you've never owned a WordPress blog before, all you have to do is to google "free WordPress tutorials" and you'll find everything you need online.

***

To help you dive right into making the most out of your self-hosted WordPress blog, I've also put together a quick checklist of things you need to do to complete the set-up of your blog:

1. Make sure your username is NOT "admin" when selecting your WordPress login details.
2. Have a really strong password that has letters, numbers and special characters and isn't a regular word.
3. After installation, delete all the plugins that came pre-installed including "JETPACK" (there are better alternatives out there, and this one is known for making your website slower). The only one that I would leave is Akismet (an anti-spam plugin).
4. Install a security plugin right away. I recommend WordFence.
5. Your hosting provider most likely has daily backups, but the more backups you have the better. So install a backup plugin. I recommend UpdraftPlus.
6. If your site will have a lot of images, I recommend using a plugin like WP Smush to optimize images. It reduces the size of your images automatically, without compromising on the image quality.

7. Install a caching plugin. I like WP Super Cache. This is vital to improving your site speed.
8. If you have a blog, make sure your posts can be easily shared across social media platforms. I like Social Warfare and it's well worth going pro (but the free version is pretty awesome as well!).

If you're looking for more must-have WordPress plugins or if you want to design your own homepage (like I did for my website), here are a few more advanced posts that are worth bookmarking:

- **10 Must-Have WordPress Plugins For Bloggers** – www.thesheapproach.com/must-have-wordpress-plugins-bloggers/
- **How To Create Free Landing Pages In WordPress** – www.thesheapproach.com/create-free-landing-pages-wordpress/

By the end of this chapter (or hopefully this week), you should know your way around WordPress enough to make relevant changes and start filling up your blog with content.

Note: To access your website, just add "wp-admin" at the end of your blog's URL to log in. For example: www.BLOGTITLE.com/wp-admin/. (You can also access it from your Bluehost account.)

PUBLISHING CONTENT

Now that your website is all pretty, you need to start publishing content for it to stop looking like a ghost town.

There are 3 main types of content that you need to have on your website: pages, posts, and menus (menus are the navigation bars that you find at the very top of the websites, containing links to different sections of that website or blog).

The main pages that your website needs are: your "About Me" page, a contact page, a privacy policy page and, if you decide on it, a static homepage.

For example, if you visit my website, www.thesheapproach.com, instead of the default theme homepage, I created my own landing page to showcase the most important aspects of what people need to know, and only added one section that shows my latest 6 blog posts.

***

Before you launch your blog, you will also need to start working on your first few blog posts.

I recommend having at least 5-6 blog posts written when you launch so that people have something to read when they visit your website for the first time.

This will also help you make a good first impression and give your readers an idea about what your blog will be about (and what it can do for them, which is what they will want to know.)

Ideally, if you choose to blog about a certain topic and you have 3 subtopics in mind (for example you're starting a parenting blog with a focus on pregnancy, breastfeeding and kid's activities or a lifestyle blog with a focus on summer style, hair tutorials and DIY fashion), you want to make sure that you have at least 1 (if not 2) blog posts written for each of these sub-categories.

This way, readers will know right away what they can expect from you. (Of course, in time you can add to these or even change your mind, but if you want to make a strong first impression, readers need to understand right away what you're all about.)

Keep in mind that these posts need to solve a problem for your target audience and they need to reflect your expertize or experience in these fields.

***

The next thing you need to focus on when putting your website together (if you haven't already) is your navigation and user accessibility.

First of all, all your posts must be categorized properly and those categories need to be easy to find.

This will be helpful to people who might only be interested in 1 or 2 of the things you write about. And to offer them a good user experience, you need to make it crazy easy for them to find whatever they are looking for on your website.

You also want to add all other relevant pages (like the ones mentioned above) to your website's menu because, ideally, if somebody wants to find a page on your blog, it shouldn't take them longer then 2 clicks for them to access it.

So keep user experience in mind, and make good use of your menus and your sidebar to showcase your blog categories, recent posts and other important sections of your website.

OTHER BLOGGING TIPS FOR BEGINNERS

Once you've done all that, there are a few other things you need to set up in preparation for growing your blog and making money from it.

Here's what you shouldn't forget to do next:

- **Secure the social media handles for your blog name.** Try, as much as possible, to keep them simple, without adding numbers, underscores or other elements.
- **Brand your blog and create a logo.** (Find out how over at www.thesheapproach.com/brand-your-blog-logo-design/) Help your blog stand out by creating a strong brand, not only around yourself but also around your blog.
- **Start taking blog photos or use free stock photos.** (If you blog about anything visual such as fashion, beauty, food and so on, taking and using your own photos is crucial, not only for your social media accounts but for your blog as well. If, however, your blog doesn't need original visual aids (you blog about finance, business, parenting etc.) you can use free stock photos or purchase

photos online to make sure your content stands out more. (In that case, you should focus a lot more on the quality of content.)

- **Install Google Analytics to track visitors**. (Find out how over at www.thesheapproach.com/bloggers-guide-google-analytics/) This is crucial to track the progress of your blog, find out more about who your audience really is and gain insight into what efforts are paying off and generating your blog traffic.
- **Submit your website to Google's Webmasters Tool.** While a bit technical, this is yet another step you don't want to miss, as it will help your website get indexed faster by search engines, as well as offer you the terms and keywords that your blog ranks for and gets clicks from.
- **Start an email list (for free).** (Find out how over at www.thesheapproach.com/start-manage-grow-email-list/) I truly believe that you can make money blogging even with a small audience, as long as this audience is engaged. Capturing visitor's email address and being able to keep in touch with them, build that like-know-and-trust factor and offer value even outside of your blog will turn your readers into loyal fans that will end up buying from you.

There is a lot more that goes into building a successful blog, but these suggestions should get you started on the right path.

If you need more help or support, I publish weekly blog posts on www.thesheapproach.com to help new and experienced bloggers grow their online presence and unlock their blog's full potential.

I cover everything from blog traffic and social media tips, to affiliate and email marketing, and go in more detail about how to tackle each one.

But keep in mind, that at least in the beginning, your blog might need a little extra time and effort to take off.

And you might not see results right away, but that doesn't mean that you're not making progress.

You need to be consistent and persistent with it in order to succeed and strive to find what makes your platform and voice unique.

CHAPTER 3: HOW TO MAKE MONEY BLOGGING

INTRODUCTION

Starting a blog with a clear vision in mind that you want it to be profitable can make you a lot more strategic in the way you approach blogging, which can be an asset.

But if you've never blogged before, you can easily get lost in the strategy and forget about the writing part. I believe that before you learn how to monetize your website, you should know how to blog first.

I recommend taking the first few weeks to focus on your blogging skills, finding your writing voice, developing your interests and growing your audience because they are vital elements to building a solid foundation first.

But nonetheless, I'm here to deliver on my promise and show you how you can make money blogging, how to create a blog monetization strategy that will work for your unique blog and blog topic, and how to grow your audience and earnings so you can build a profitable blog.

THE BEST WAY TO MAKE MONEY BLOGGING

To help you figure out how real bloggers make money online, I'm going to break down all the ways in which you can monetize a website so you can choose the best method, according to your niche and your audience.

Because here's a little behind-the-scenes insight into the blogging world, there is not just 1 correct way to make money blogging. Different bloggers monetize in different ways, and most of them combine 2 or 3 of these methods to generate profit in a proactive way.

I've created a free quiz that you can take to discover which method will work the best for where you are now in your blogging journey, and I invite you to take it.

You can find it by typing in www.thesheapproach.com/quiz in your browser.

But in this chapter, I will walk you through everything you need to know about how real bloggers make money today so you can make a decision based on your blog and your blogging goals.

AD DISPLAY

One of the first ways you can monetize your blog that is quite popular (but not very lucrative) is by displaying ads on your blog.

This method really pays off if you have crazy amounts of traffic and website visitors, so it's not the best strategy for new bloggers, but it can be a good passive income source once your blog starts growing.

The way it works is quite straightforward: you join ad networks such as Google Adsense, Ad Thrive or Mediavine, place their ads on your website and you get paid per impressions (the amount of times someone sees an ad) or clicks, depending on the network.

You can get started with earning money from ads by reading my post on How To Get Your

First Google Adsense Payment that you an find over at www.thesheapproach.com/first-google-adsense-payment/.

To give you an idea of what you can earn, a few bloggers I know have reported making:

- $10-20 per day with 1,000 daily page views
- $250 per month with over 30,000 sessions
- $550 per month with 45,000 page views
- $2000 per month with over 170,000 page views
- $5480 per month with 312,394 page views

Keep in mind that page views are counted individually while sessions are tracked from the moment someone arrives on your website until they leave.

For example, if I visit your blog and look at 5 different blog posts or pages, that's the equivalent of 1 session and 5 page views.

Reaching that amount of traffic is hard work and it's going to take time. I recommend starting off with Google Adsense and applying to other networks such as Mediavine and Ad Thrive when you reach 25k and, respectively, 100k monthly sessions. (That's the minimum amount of traffic you need to have to be accepted in those bigger networks.)

But if you want to start earning money from ad networks one thing is for sure, you need to grow your blog traffic and you need to do it fast.

If you want to learn how I went from 0 to 50,000 page views (and beyond) as a new blogger, check out my eBook: <u>The She Approach To Boosting Your Blog Traffic</u> over at <u>www.thesheapproach.com/boost-blog-traffic/</u>.

I wrote this eBook with beginners in mind, so everything you need to know about promoting a new blog (such as what social media share buttons to add to your blog, how to master different social media channels, how to grow your blog with the help of an email list, what is SEO and how to leverage it, and a lot more) is included here.

There's only so much I can add in this eBook, but increasing your blog traffic should be a top priority once you decide on how you want to monetize because, in almost every situation, more traffic will equal more income.

AFFILIATE MARKETING

Affiliate marketing is a much better way to make money with a new blog because you can earn a lot more with the same small audience. In fact, if you've read any of my income reports, you probably know that this is the main way I monetize my blog.

Affiliate marketing is the process of promoting certain companies, products or brands, and receiving a commission when someone makes a purchase through one of your links.

To get started with affiliate marketing and learn more about how it works, you can enroll in my 5-day email video course by going over to www.thesheapproach.com/free-affiliate-marketing-course/. (It's free and it has a lot of useful information!)

You can become an affiliate for pretty much everything under the sun, including online retailers like Amazon and Walmart, smaller boutique stores and even become affiliated with digital products and service sellers.

Because these companies only have to pay you when you make a sale, they allow even new bloggers to join their affiliate programs, so that means you can get started with it as soon as your blog is live and you have some content up as well.

For more information on affiliate marketing, I invite you to browse through my blog posts on this topic over at www.thesheapproach.com/category/affiliate-marketing-tips/.

I find affiliate marketing an amazing way to monetize any blog because it offers you the opportunity to present your readers with different solutions for the problems they are facing (and you don't have to create, store or ship any of those products or resources yourself).

If you want to get started with affiliate marketing right away, check out my Affiliate Marketing Training Bundle For Beginners over at www.thesheapproach.com/affiliate-marketing-training-bundle/.

This training was designed to help new and inexperienced bloggers make their first $1,000 in affiliate sales and it contains everything you need to understand and master affiliate marketing (including video trainings, access to a Facebook community and case studies on real and successful affiliate campaigns where I show you exactly how I did it).

A lot of modern bloggers seem to overlook affiliate marketing, which I consider to be a big mistake, considering the fact that once you've included an affiliate link in the right place, you can earn from it on an undetermined period of time as long as people find and use that link.

In comparison to that, working with brands to write blog posts, which I'll cover next, only pays once and you put in the same amount of work, while affiliate marketing can be easily scalable and much more passive.

SPONSORED POSTS

Another popular way to make money blogging is to work with brands and create sponsored posts (either on your blog or social media channels) in exchange for either free products or (ideally) a monetary compensation.

In essence, brands that are looking to promote their products through content marketing or generate more traffic, sales or brand exposure, will often work with influencers and bloggers.

For brands to be willing to compensate you for your efforts (rather than just offering free products), you need to have quite a big following and quality content.

You also need to learn to reach out to brands and pitch them your ideas instead of just waiting to be magically contacted by them.

If you're looking to get started and work with brands, I recommend joining a few influencer networks (they connect contact creators to brands) such as Social Native, Activate, Fame Bit and so on.

Consider preparing a media kit to showcase your blogs, your rates and your relevant blog statistics (most brands require it) and create quality content on your blog in order to be considered for campaigns.

You can also create a "Work With Me" page on your blog to invite brands to contact you, and list the type of collaborations you would be open to.

Keeping an eye out for opportunities to work with brands is also a great idea. For example, if you search the #BloggersRequired hashtag on Twitter, you will often see PR requests from brands who are looking to discover new blogs.

And if you see other bloggers working with brands that you'd love to work with as well, contact and pitch to them!

The truth is, that due to the nature of my niche, sponsored posts are not something I do often (but the fact that I still got contacted by relevant software companies to do them, just proves that there is an opportunity out there for everyone, no matter what topic they cover!) or something that I consider myself much of an expert on.

But it can be quite lucrative, with brands paying anywhere between $200 to $500 per collaboration (depending on the size of your blog and your social reach), so if you want to learn more about it, I highly recommend checking out this course on How To Find And Pitch For Sponsored Posts that you can access over at www.thesheapproach.com/sponsored.

It was created by one of my blogging friends who has a lot more success when it comes to working with brands and it's jam-packed with valuable information that will save you a lot of time.

SELLING DIGITAL PRODUCTS

The last way bloggers make money online is by selling digital products, also known as info-products (such as e-courses, eBooks, printables, cheat sheets, video lessons, and so on).

If your chosen blog niche cannot be monetized in any of the other ways I mentioned, then I do recommend coming up with a product idea to share your expertize with your audience and help them solve a unique problem.

I recommend starting with something small, like an eBook, and then moving on to create bigger digital products that you can price higher.

Digital products are a great source of passive income because you create them once and they are automatically delivered to the buyers without you having to lift another finger (as long as you have the right systems in place, which are so easy to set up).

In particular, eBooks are easy to create and they allow you to take your readers on a transformational journey where you can share so much more than you could in a blog post. And because you're offering so much more value on a topic that you have a lot of knowledge on, your readers are willing to pay for it.

If you want to get started with writing and launching your first eBook, I have an entire blog post series on this topic, starting with a post on "The Quickest Way To Write Your First Ebook" over at www.thesheapproach.com/quickest-way-write-first-ebook/ that will explain the benefits on having a digital product for sale, along with how you can make it happen.

In the second blog post of the series, "How To Publish, Launch And Sell Your First Ebook", I dive in deeper on how you can publish and sell eBooks (or other digital products) on your website (or on Amazon) to generate extra revenue in your blogging business.

Find part 2 over at www.thesheapproach.com/publish-launch-sell-first-ebook/.

And, because selling digital products isn't second nature for us, but something that has to be learned, I've also shared my best tips on how to sell your eBook after you launch it part 3 of the blog post series titled "How To Make Passive Income By Selling eBooks".

Read part 3 over at www.thesheapproach.com/how-to-generate-passive-income-by-selling-ebooks/.

But having digital products for sales has changed everything for my blog and, knowing what I know now, I just wish I started creating and selling them sooner.

HOW TO FORM A BLOG MONETIZATION STRATEGY

Now that you know all the ways in which you can make money blogging, you need to come up with a strategy to tackle the relevant methods that could be applied to you and get started.

It all comes down to the opportunities in your niche. For example, beauty and lifestyle bloggers have a lot of opportunities to work with brands, while business bloggers tend to do really well with affiliate marketing because there are a lot of courses or resources they can promote.

But I also know DIY bloggers who work with brands or food bloggers who earn a lot selling online courses.

And that's because every blog is different and nowadays there are more opportunities than ever to monetize your blog in multiple ways.

That being said, I highly believe that in order to be profitable, you have to diversify your income.

You can't expect to make a full-time living by only placing ads on your blog. So keep your options open and test out all the methods (one at a time) to find out what works best for you.

***

If you're just starting out, I would focus on affiliate marketing and creating a digital product first. As you grow your traffic and your audience, leverage that to introduce ads and brand sponsorships as well if they are relevant to your niche.

Because I know how easy it is to get carried away and try to do everything at once, I recommend that you start and work on one method each month.

Master that, look at how other bloggers in your niche are doing it and then do it better by using the tips and tricks I've shared in this eBook.

Don't be afraid to strike out or fail and if something doesn't work right away, figure out why. Is there anything you could do better? Or is it just not possible for you to monetize your blog that way?

It took me 4 months to make my first affiliate sale (a whopping $7), but if I had given up on affiliate marketing without giving it a real shot and without trying new strategies, I would probably not be writing this eBook right now.

So don't write off any methods until you're absolutely certain that they won't work for you.

***

Making a plan of how much you want to earn blogging and in which ways you want to generate it can also help you be focused on how you're going make it happen.

For example, if you want to make 5% of your blogging income with ads, 75% with affiliate marketing and 20% with brand sponsorships, it will soon become clear what you need to focus on each month.

Will you prioritize creating content? Reaching out to brands? Growing your traffic or a certain social media platform? You can't do it all at once, so divide and conquer.

***

I also recommend keeping track of everything you earn from your blog, not only for tax purposes but so you can see your progress, figure out what's working and what you need to improve.

I use a Google Spreadsheet, and keep track of every payment that I receive (and everything I invest in my blog as well), along with other statistics about my blog such as traffic, email subscribers, social media followers and anything else that's relevant to my business.

In doing so, I am able to analyze what's going on in my blog, adapt, make improvements and track my progress, which are all important pieces of the puzzle when you treat your blog as a business.

CONCLUSION

If you're still undecided or unsure about the best way to monetize YOUR blog (because, as I already said, all blogs are different), don't forget to take my free quiz.

> ➤ www.thesheapproach.com/quiz

But your best bet will be to combine at least 2 (if not more) of these income sources and experiment with as many as possible to see what works for you.

And don't forget to add value to your audience regardless of what path you're going to take. Don't promote brands that are irrelevant to your blog topic, don't overload your website with ads and don't say yes to everything that comes your way.

Learn to be picky, and keep your focus on building trust with your audience if you ever want them to buy from you.

And above all, be consistent and try to put only your best work out there. You need to show up, even when things don't look like they are moving in the right direction, offer a lot of value to your readers and look for ways to improve your strategy and content where and when you can.

I wrote this eBook because I'm so excited to see more and more opportunities for bloggers to make money online, and for everyday people to follow their dreams and build a digital business.

If you told me two years ago that today I would be making money with a small blog and I would be paid to bring my inner digital geek out, I would've probably called you crazy. But here I am, living proof that this can work!

And trust me, there's nothing special about me. The only reason why I "made it" is because I'm stubborn. I saw it working for other people and I thought to myself: "if they can do it, so can I".

Now the ball is in your court and you have a responsibility to share your awesomeness with the world. Start that blog, build that online business and follow your passion! Your future self will thank you.

For more resources , eBooks by me and affiliate marketing trainings, check out my digital shop over at www.thesheaapproach.com/shop

ABOUT THE AUTHOR

Ana Savuica is the blogging growth strategist and coach behind The She Approach where she empowers women to build their digital empires by offering actionable tips and easy-to-implement strategies on how to tackle blogging and online marketing.

In particular, she teaches bloggers how to get started, increase their traffic and income, build an engaged audience and profit from their passion.

After working behind the scenes for several e-commerce companies, Ana started her own blog in 2016 and has since grown it into a profitable online venture, but her true passion is to help other women blog with purpose and see real results.

If you need personalized advice and someone to keep you accountable to make your blogging dreams a reality, you can check out Ana's 1-on-1 coaching services and hire her as your blogging coach over at www.thesheapproach.com/private-blog-coaching/.

She has been featured in prestigious online publications such as the Social Media Examiner, hosted workshops in collaboration with Google's Digital Garage initiative in the UK and spoke at blogger events such as Blog Con London.

Ana is also the founder of Blogging Mode an online gift shop for bloggers and entrepreneurs, where she celebrates online creatives and creators.

You can get in touch with her by visiting her website, following her on Instagram @thesheapproach or on Facebook at www.facebook.com/thesheapproach.

And, if you want more exclusive and advanced blogging tips, don't forget to sign up for The She Approach newsletter over at: welcome.thesheapproach.com or on her website at www.thesheapproach.com.

BLOG BRAINSTORMING WORKSHEETS

1. WHY do you want to start this blog? List 3-5 reasons that motivate you.

2. List 3-5 topics that you're really passionate about and would love to cover on your blog.

3. What topics could you give a one-jour presentation on without any preparation? List 3-5 topics that you have a lot of knowledge, experience or expertise in.

4. Pick out your blog niche! Decide on 1,2 or maximum 3 topics (with appropriate sub-topics) that you're going to cover on your blog and list them below.

5. Who is your target audience? Based on the niche you've chosen, who are the people that would be considered your ideal readers? List them below in as much detail as possible.

6. Brainstorm 5-10 possible blog name ideas. Double-check if they are taken and pick the one that speaks to you the most.

7. Come up with a short tagline that best describes your blog's mission.

8. Where do you want your blog to be in 6 months? Write down an overview of your blogging goals and the steps you'll need to take to get there:

BUILD YOUR WEBSITE CHECKLIST

- ☐ Buy hosting. Go to www.thesheapproach.com/bluehost to get the best deal
- ☐ Follow your host's instructions and install WordPress on your website
- ☐ Find and install a professional WordPress theme
- ☐ Install all the relevant plugins (a security plugin, a back-up plugin etc)
- ☐ Find and install a social media sharing plugin
- ☐ Set up your "About", "Contact me" and "Privacy Policy" pages
- ☐ Write and publish at least 5 blog posts
- ☐ Organize your blog posts into categories and create your main website menu
- ☐ Secure the social media handles for your blog name
- ☐ Create a logo for your blog and plan out your branding and your color scheme
- ☐ Start taking or sourcing your blog images
- ☐ Install Google Analytics and set up Google Webmasters
- ☐ Start an email list for free. Go to www.thesheapproach.com/mailerlite

BLOG MONETIZATION STRATEGY

Read the last chapter again and figure out what's the best way to monetize your blog.

Plan out accordingly and fill out the following boxes to get clear on your action plan. Then use the "Notes" section at the end of this book to map out your masterplan even further.

1. The top two ways in which you are going to make money blogging are...

2. The first strategy that you're going to focus on, learn more about, and implement first is ... (either affiliate marketing, ads, sponsored post or digital products)

3. You want to make your first $100 by...

4. You want to make your first $1,000 blogging by ....

5. To make that happen, you will need to... (list a few tasks + strategies that you're going to have to complete in order to achieve those results – for example: "*reach out to 5 brands and work on 2 sponsored posts*" or "*get good at Pinterest, reach 20k page views/month and get accepted into a bigger ad network*")

NOTES

60583314R00052

Made in the USA
Columbia, SC
15 June 2019